I0166165

Orsamus Holmes Marshall

The Niagara Frontier

Orsamus Holmes Marshall

The Niagara Frontier

ISBN/EAN: 9783743345171

Manufactured in Europe, USA, Canada, Australia, Japa

Cover: Foto ©ninafisch / pixelio.de

Manufactured and distributed by brebook publishing software
(www.brebook.com)

Orsamus Holmes Marshall

The Niagara Frontier

THE

NIAGARA FRONTIER.

EMBRACING

SKETCHES OF ITS EARLY HISTORY,

AND

Indian, French and English Local Names.

READ BEFORE THE BUFFALO HISTORICAL SOCIETY,

FEBRUARY 27TH, 1865,

BY ORSAMUS H. MARSHALL.

Reprinted for private circulation from the Publications of the Buffalo Historical Society.

1881.

THE
NIAGARA FRONTIER.

EMBRACING SKETCHES OF ITS EARLY HISTORY, AND INDIAN, FRENCH
AND ENGLISH LOCAL NAMES.

READ BEFORE THE SOCIETY, FEBRUARY 27, 1865.

BY ORSAMUS H. MARSHALL.

JAMES CARTIER, while exploring the Gulf of St. Lawrence in
1535, was informed by the savages, living on its borders, that
a mighty river, which they called Hochelaga, flowed into the
sea near by, from a vast distance in the interior.* Having discovered its mouth, he explored the stream as far as the site of
the present City of Montreal. He inquired of the Indians
whom he met on the way, touching the source of that great
river and the country through which it flowed. He was told,
that after ascending many leagues among rapids and water-falls,
he would reach a lake, one hundred and fifty leagues long and
forty or fifty broad, at the western extremity of which the
waters were wholesome and the winters mild; that a river emptied into it from the south, which had its source in the country
of the Iroquois; that beyond this lake he would find a cataract
and portage; then another lake about equal to the former,
which they had never explored; and, still further on, a sea, the

---

* Lescarbot, p. 300

western shores of which they had never seen, nor had they heard of any one who had.*

This is the earliest historical notice of our great lake region.

Cartier was followed, after a long interval, by French traders, adventurers and missionaries; who, stimulated by love of adventure or the attractions of the fur trade, or inspired by religious zeal, were the first to penetrate the Canadian wilderness, and encounter the privations and dangers incident to the exploration of the vast interior of North America.

Before the Pilgrims landed in New England, Champlain had wintered among the savages on the eastern shore of Lake Huron, and had crossed Lake Ontario with an expedition against the Iroquois in the central part of our State.†

As one after another of the principal lakes and rivers of the New World were discovered, they were called in honor of some tutelary saint or patron, some king or noble. The early travelers not only rejected their aboriginal names, but, in many instances, failed even to mention them. The series of lakes on our northern border, were originally considered as expansions of one continuous river, called by the old geographers Saint Lawrence, in honor of the martyr, on the day of whose festival the noble gulf at its outlet was discovered.

During the three centuries which have elapsed since that event took place, two distinct races have successively occupied and disappeared from this locality, now in the undisputed possession of a third.

The traveler in the classic regions of the Old World, encounters, at every step, venerable monuments and crumbling ruins; silent but eloquent memorials of those who have risen, flourished, and disappeared in the revolutions of time. The Indian, once lord of this New World, now a tenant at the will of the white man, was skilled in none but the rudest arts. He roamed, a child of nature, over the forest and prairie, absorbed

---

* Lescarbot, p. 381.
† Voyages de Champlain, Part i. p. 251.   Edition of 1632.

in his ceaseless struggle for a precarious subsistence on the fruits of the chase. He built no monuments and has left no records, from which we may learn the story of his origin, his migrations, his bloody wars and fruitless conquests. The only light which shines upon his annals, is, at best, a dim and shadowy tradition. Scarce a memorial of his former occupancy remains, save the *names* he has bestowed upon the lakes, rivers, and prominent landmarks of the country. The Iroquois dialects still live in their melodious geographical terms, suggesting a sad contrast between their former proud and extensive dominion and their present feeble and reduced condition.

There is no satisfactory evidence of the existence, in this vicinity, of a race preceding the Indians. The "mound-builders," that mysterious people who once spread in countless multitudes over the valleys of the Ohio, the Mississippi, and their tributaries, never, so far as diligent research has been able to discover, dwelt in this locality. The ancient fortifications, tumuli, and artificial structures that abound in Western New York, can all be referred to a later date and a more modern race. But at what precise period, and by what particular people they were constructed, are questions which have hitherto eluded the most diligent historical research. The Senecas are equally ignorant on this subject. The venerable Seneca White, a distinguished Iroquois chief residing on the Cattaraugus Reservation, now eighty-one years old,* expressed his curiosity on the subject, in a recent interview with the writer; and desired to know when, why and by whom those structures had been built. Many of them may yet be seen within a few miles of our city, and are certainly objects of historical interest and speculation.

Omitting, therefore, from necessity, any notice of the race, of whom these remains are the only memorial, we find that the first in this locality, of whom history makes mention, were the

---

* He died since the above was written, on the nineteenth of May, 1873.—ED.

Attiouandaronk, or Neutral Nation, called Kah-kwas by the Senecas.* They had their council-fires along the Niagara, but principally on its western side. Their hunting-grounds extended from the Genesee nearly to the eastern shores of Lake Huron, embracing a wide and important territory. In this region, now teeming with Anglo-Saxon life, they reared their rude wigwams, pursued their game, and preserved a rigid and singular neutrality between the fierce tribes that waged their bloody wars on all sides around them. They are first mentioned by Champlain during his winter visit to the Hurons in 1615, before alluded to, but he was unable to visit their territory. According to the early Jesuits, they excelled the Hurons in stature, strength, and symmetry, and wore their dress with a superior grace. They regarded their dead with peculiar veneration. Once in every ten years the survivors of each family gathered the remains of their deceased ancestors from the platforms on which they had been deposited, and buried them in heaps, with many superstitious ceremonies. This was called the "Feast of the Dead." Many of the mounds thus raised may still be seen in this vicinity. A conspicuous one on Tonawanda Island, is affirmed by the old Senecas to have had such an origin. The land of the Neutral Nation is described by the Jesuits as producing an abundance of corn, beans, and other vegetables; their rivers as abounding in fish of endless variety, and their forests as filled with a profusion of game, yielding the richest furs.

The peace which this peculiar people had so long maintained with the Iroquois was destined to be broken. Some jealousies and collisions occurred in 1647, which culminated in open war in 1650. One of the villages of the Neutral Nation, nearest the Senecas and not far from the site of our city, was

---

* It has been assumed by many writers that the Kah-kwas and Eries were identical. This is not so. The latter, according to the most reliable authorities, lived south of the western extremity of Lake Erie until they were destroyed by the Iroquois, in 1655. The Kah-kwas were exterminated by them as early as 1651. On Coronelli's map, published in 1688, one of the villages of the latter, called "Kakouagoga, *a destroyed nation*," is located at or near the site of Buffalo.

captured in the autumn of the latter year, and another the ensuing spring.* So well-directed and energetic were the blows
of the Iroquois, that the total destruction of the Neutral Nation was speedily accomplished. All the old men and children,
who were unable to follow their captors, were put to death;
but the women were reserved to supply the waste occasioned
by the war. The survivors were adopted by their conquerors;
and, as late as 1669, a small remnant was found by the Jesuit,
Father Fremin, living within the limits of the present County
of Ontario.

Such were the predecessors of the Senecas. A little more
than two centuries has elapsed since they lived and flourished
in this locality, and no evidence of their occupancy now exists,
save the rude mounds which mark their final resting-places.
Scarce a trace of their language remains, and we know only
that they spoke a dialect kindred to that of the Senecas.
Blotted out from among the nations, they have left one conspicuous and enduring memorial of their existence, in the
name of the beautiful and noble river that divides their ancient domain.†

A long period intervened between the destruction of the
Neutral Nation and the permanent occupation of their country by the Senecas. For more than a century, this beautiful
region was abandoned to the undisturbed dominion of nature,
save when traversed by the warrior on his predatory errand,
or the hunter in pursuit of game. A dense and unexplored
wildernesss extended from the Genesee to the Niagara; with
but here and there an interval, where the oak openings let in
the sunlight, or the prairie lured the deer and the elk to crop
its luxuriant herbage.

The Senecas continued to live east of the Genesee, in four
principal villages, until the year 1687, when the Marquis de
Nonville, then Governor of Canada, invaded their country

* Relation des Jesuites, 1651, p. 4.
† See " Last of the Kah-Kwas," vol. i., p. 43.—ED.

with a powerful army; and, after defeating them near the site of Victor, in Ontario County, drove them from their burning villages and laid waste their territories.* The humbled Senecas, influenced by superstition, never rebuilt a solitary cabin. Their abandoned homes long bore witness to that most disastrous era in the history of the Confederacy. We next find them in scattered villages on the banks of their favorite Jenis'-hi-yuh;† in the fertile valley of which they resumed the cultivation of the maize, and recovered, in some degree, their former power and influence.

During the Revolutionary War they espoused the British cause. The atrocities they committed in their savage mode of warfare, culminated in 1778 in the memorable massacre at Wyoming; and induced General Washington, in imitation of De Nonville, to send an army for their chastisement. The famous expedition under General Sullivan was organized for this purpose in 1779; which, penetrating the heart of the Seneca country, resulted, for the time being, in their overthrow and complete dispersion. The proud and formidable nation fled, panic-stricken, from their "pleasant valley," abandoned their villages, and sought British protection under the guns of Fort Niagara. They never, as a nation, resumed their ancient seats along the Genesee, but sought and found a new home on the secluded banks and among the basswood forests of the Do'-syo-wä, or ~Buffalo Creek, whence they had driven the Neutral Nation one hundred and thirty years before.

I have thus, with as much brevity as the nature of my subject would admit, noticed the aboriginal races that preceded us in the occupancy of this region. I consider this as an appropriate introduction to a historical sketch of the most prominent localities on the Niagara frontier, and of the various names by which they have been known.

---

* N. Y. Historical Collection, Second Series, vol. ii., p. 180.
† Or Genesee, signifying *beautiful, pleasant valley.* The key to the pronunciation of the Seneca names will be found in the Appendix.

On the sixth day of December, 1678, a brigantine of ten tons, doubled the point where Fort Niagara now stands, and anchored in the sheltered waters of the river.* It had been sent at that inclement season from Fort Frontenac, now Kingston, by the Sieur de la Salle, in prosecution of the bold enterprises conceived by that intrepid discoverer, involving the exploration of a vast and unknown country, in vessels built on the way. The crew consisted of sixteen persons, under the command of the Sieur de la Motte. *"Te Deum laudamus!"* arose from the deck of the vessel, as it entered the noble river. The strains of that ancient hymn of the church as they echoed from shore and forest, must have startled the watchful Senecas as they gazed upon their strange visitors. Never before had white man, so far as history tells us, ascended the river. On its borders, the roving Indian still contended for supremacy with the scarce wilder beasts of the forest. All was yet primitive and unexplored. Dense woods overhung the banks, except at the site of the present fort, or at the Indian village opposite, where a few temporary cabins sheltered some fishing-parties of the Senecas. The stream in which the French were now anchored, they called by its Indian name, Niagara. It is the oldest of all the local geographical terms which have come down to us from the aborigines. It was not at first thus written by the English; for with them it passed through almost every possible alphabetical variation before its present orthography was established.† We find its germ in the On-gui-aah-ra of the Neutral Nation, as given by Father L'Allemant, in a letter dated in 1641, at the mission-station of Sainte Marie, on Lake Huron. In describing his visit to that people, he says: "From their first village, which is about forty leagues southerly from Sainte Marie, it is four days' travel in a southeasterly direction, to where the celebrated river of the

---

* Hennepin, p. 74, Edition of 1698.
† *Thirty-nine* different modes of spelling Niagara are enumerate l by Dr. O' allaghan N. Y. Colonial Documents, Index Volume, p. 465.

Neutral Nation empties into Lake Ontario. On the west and not on the eastern side of said river, are the principal villages of that nation. There are three or four on the eastern side, extending from east to west toward the Eries or Cat Nation. This river," he adds, "is that by which our great lake of the Hurons is discharged, after having emptied into Lake Erie, or Lake of the Cat Nation, and it takes the name of On-gui-aah-ra, until it empties into Ontario or St. Louis Lake."[*]

The name of the river next occurs on Sanson's map of Canada, published in Paris in 1656 where it is spelled "Ongiara." Its first appearance as Niagara, is on Coronelli's map, published in Paris in 1688. From that time to the present, the French have been consistent in their orthography, the numerous variations alluded to, occurring only among English writers. The word was probably derived from the Mohawks, through whom the French had their first intercourse with the Iroquois. The Mohawks pronounce it Nyah'-ga-rah', with the primary accent on the first syllable, and the secondary on the last. Some controversy has existed concerning its signification. It is probably the same both in the Neutral and Mohawk languages, as they were kindred dialects of one generic tongue. The Mohawks affirm it to mean *neck*, in allusion to its connecting the two lakes. The corresponding Seneca name, Nyah'-gaah,[†] was always confined by the Iroquois to the section of the river below the Falls, and to Lake Ontario. That portion of the river above. the Falls[‡] being sometimes called Gai-gwääh-gĕh, -one of their names for Lake Erie.

The name Niagara was sometimes applied, by the early historians, not only to the river, but to a defensive work and group of Indian cabins, which stood at or near the site of the present Village of Lewiston. La Salle constructed, at this point, a cabin of palisades to serve as a magazine or storehouse.

* Relation, 1641, p. 71.
† The signification of this Seneca word is lost. It is probably derived from the name conferred by the Neutral Nation.
‡ N. Y. Colonial Documents, vol. v., p. 800, and ix., p. 999.

In order to allay the jealousies which the work excited among the Senecas, he sent an embassy to Tegarondies, the principal village of the confederacy, then located on what is now known as Boughton Hill, near Victor, in Ontario County. They reached it in five days, after a march in mid-winter of thirty-two leagues, on snowshoes, during which they subsisted only on parched corn. There they found the Jesuits, Garnier and Raffeix, who had been resident missionaries since 1669. A council was held with the Senecas, and presents interchanged, but without favorable result. The French retraced their steps to their camp on the river, worn out with the hardships of the way, and glad to exchange their meager diet for the delicious white-fish just then in season.*

No regular defensive work was constructed in the vicinity, until the Marquis De Nonville, on his return from the expedition before alluded to, fortified the tongue of land which lies between the lake and river, and thus founded the present fort. The French General describes the position as "the most beautiful, pleasing and advantageous on the whole lake." As early as 1686, he had proposed to his Government to erect a stone structure at this point, sufficient for a garrison of five hundred men, but received no favorable response. Many difficulties were encountered in the erection of the new fortress. As the place was barren of suitable wood, palisades were cut at a distance, floated to the adjacent beach, and drawn up, with great labor, to the top of the bank. The work was finally completed, and called, after its founder, Fort De Nonville. It subsequently appears on some of the maps as Fort Conty, after a prince of that name, who was a patron of Tonti, one of La Salle's companions; but Niagara soon became its exclusive and more appropriate designation. De Nonville left in the fort a garrison of one hundred men who were compelled by sickness to abandon it the following season, after having partially de-

---

* For a detailed account of this expedition, by the same author, see vol. i., p. 260.—ED.

stroyed it. They left many of its buildings in a habitable condition, as may be learned from a curious inventory and statement drawn up at the time of the evacuation.* No measures appear to have been taken for its reconstruction until 1725; when, by consent of the Iroquois, it was commenced in stone, and finished the following year. The "old mess-house" is a relic of that year.

The French having, through the influence of Joncaire, obtained the consent of the Senecas, rebuilt their store-house at Lewiston in 1719–20. It formed a block-house forty feet long, by thirty wide, enclosed with palisades, musket-proof, and pierced with port-holes. Around this nucleus gathered a cluster of ten Seneca cabins; and patches of corn, beans, squashes and melons were soon under cultivation. Father Charlevoix visited the spot in 1721, while on his extensive tour along the lakes; and has left quite an exaggerated description of the ridge at Lewiston, which he calls "a frightful mountain, that hides itself in the clouds, on which the Titans might attempt to scale the heavens!"†

The block-house must have soon fallen to decay, for we find Louis XV. proposing to rebuild it in 1727,‡ but the project was abandoned the next year.

This locality was always considered an important point in the early history of the Niagara frontier. Here was the commencement of the Portage around the Falls, where all the goods in process of transportation between the lakes underwent transhipment. The traveled road pursued, as now, a zig-zag course up the mountain ridge; but the heavy goods were raised or lowered in a sliding car or cradle, moved on an inclined plane by a windlass. The remains of the old tram-way were visible at a late period, and, possibly, may still be seen. The ascent of the ledge at this point was so difficult, that long

* N. Y. Colonial Documents, vol. ix., p. 386.
† Charlevoix's Journal, vol. ii., p. 345.
‡ N. Y. Colonial Documents, vol. ix., p. 964.

before the railway was constructed, the Senecas call it Duh'-jih-heh'-oh, which signifies, literally, *walking on all fours*; in allusion to the postures assumed by the French and Indians while climbing the steep acclivity under their heavy burdens. Hennepin calls it "the three mountains," *trois montagnes,*[*] referring to the high river-bank and the two terraces above it, which form the mountain ridge. When Kalm arrived there in 1750, he found one of the Joncaires still a resident. Over two hundred Senecas were then employed in carrying furs over the portage, at the rate of twenty pence a pack for the entire distance.[†] There were three warehouses at the foot of the ridge in 1759, and one at its summit; all used for storing the goods *in transitu.*

Opposite Fort Niagara, on the Canada side of the river, is Mississauga Point, so called after one of the Algonkin tribes that formerly resided in the vicinity.[‡] The present Village of Niagara was known in 1780, by the name of Butlersbury, after Colonel Butler, of Wyoming notoriety.[§] It was afterward called Newark, after the place of that name in New Jersey, and West Niagara and British Niagara. In 1792, it became the residence of the Lieutenant-Governor of Canada, and in the autumn of that year, the first session of the Parliament of the Upper Province was held there. It is an older settlement than any on the eastern side of the river, and boasted a weekly newspaper as early as 1793.[‖] About one mile above Newark, a defensive work was built by the British, at the close of the last century, called Fort George. Between this and the river was a storehouse, bearing the high-sounding name of Navy Hall; and near the latter stood the residence of Lieutenant-Governor Simcoe.

---

* Hennepin, p. 113. Edition 1698.
† Kalm's letter in Annual Register, vol. i., p. 389.
‡ An Indian village existed here at the time of La Salle's first visit in 1679.
§ Gilbert's Narrative, p. 52. Col. Butler died in 1796. Merritt's MS.
‖ Called the Upper Canada Gazette, or, American Oracle. The first number appeared April 18, 1793.

Queenston, so called in honor of Queen Charlotte, had no earlier name, though the locality was frequently noticed by the first explorers. Hennepin speaks of it as "the great rock," *la grosse roche,** referring to an immense mass, which, becoming detached from the brow of the mountain, had fallen into the river below. It is now plainly visible under the western end of the lower suspenson bridge.

The Devil's Hole and the Whirlpool are not noticed by any of the early travelers. The former is more particularly celebrated as the scene of a well known bloody tragedy, in 1763. Its Seneca name, Dyus-dä'-nyah-goh, signifies, *the cleft rocks.*† The Bloody Run, which falls over the precipice at this point, derives its present name from the same tragic occurrence, though the Indians have no term to distinguish it from the Devil's Hole. Their name for the Whirlpool, Dyu-no'-wa-da-se', means, literally, *the current goes round.*

It has already been stated, that the Indians, whom Cartier met in the Gulf of St. Lawrence in 1535, alluded, in their description of the interior of the continent, to a "cataract and portage," at the western extremity of Lake Ontario. This is the first historical notice of Niagara Falls. Seventy-eight years afterward, Champlain published an account of his voyages in Canada, illustrated by a map of the country, on which the several lakes, as far west as Lake Huron, are laid down, though in very erroneous outline.‡ It distinctly shows the river Niagara, interrupted by a waterfall, and intersected by an elevation of land, answering to the mountain ridge at Lewiston. It contains no specific name for the cataract, but calls it *saut d'eau,* or *waterfall.* Champlain describes it as "so very high that many kinds of fish are stunned in its descent!"

The next notice of the cataract is by the Jesuit, Father Ragueneau, who, in a letter to the Superior of the Missions at

---

* Hennepin, p. 113, Edition 1688.
† The river-bank is *cleft* by the action of the Bloody Run.
‡ Edition of 1632.

Paris, dated in 1648, says, "North of the Eries is a great lake, about two hundred leagues in circumference, called *Erié*, formed by the discharge of the *mer-douce*, or Lake Huron, and which falls into a third lake, called Ontario, over a cataract of frightful height."[*]

Hennepin is the first who published a detailed description of this remarkable waterfall. He first saw it in the winter of 1678–9, and accompanies his description by an engraved sketch,[†] evidently drawn from memory, as it embraces a bird's-eye view of the whole river, as far as Lake Erie, with the *Griffon* in the distance. The two falls, with Goat Island between, and Table Rock, are very well delineated, though the height is much exaggerated. A group of Frenchmen, viewing the cataract from the American side, are represented as stopping their ears to shut out the deafening sound.

No doubt the Falls were visited at an earlier date by numerous traders and *voyageurs*, but no record of the fact exists. The Niagara was not a favorite route to the Far West, the Ottawa being shorter and safer for a canoe voyage; an easy portage connecting its head-waters with Lake Huron. The fatiguing transit around the Falls, and the hostility of the warlike Iroquois, were formidable obstacles to the more southern course.

The Senecas call the cataract, Det-ga*h*-sk*o*h-ses, signifying *the place of the high fall.* They never call it Niagara, nor by any similar term; neither does that word signify in their language *thunder of waters*, as affirmed by Schoolcraft.[‡] Such a meaning would be eminently poetic, but truth is of higher importance.

The picturesque Islands which add so much to the beauty and unrivaled scenery of the Falls, must have challenged the admiration and stimulated the curiosity of the early visitor. Equally attractive at all seasons, whether arrayed in summer

* Jesuit Relation, 1648, p. 46.
† Hennepin, p. 116, Edition of 1698.
‡ Tour to the Lakes, p. 72.

verdure, autumnal tints or winter dress,* they reposed like
fairy creations, amid the turmoil of the impetuous rapids, iso-
lated and apparently secure from human intrusion or profana-
tion.   Traditions exist of early Indian visits to the larger one,
which are confirmed by a deposit of human bones discovered
near its head.   The access was from the river above, through
the still water between the divided currents.   Judge Porter
first landed there in 1806, and found several dates carved on a
beech, the earliest of which was 1769.   He purchased the entire group from the State in 1816, and during the following
year, built the first bridge which connected them with the
main land.   Stedman had cleared a small field near the upper
end of the largest, and colonized it with a few animals, including a venerable goat.   The latter was the only survivor of the
severe winter of 1779–80, in commemoration of which the
island received its present name.   The Boundary Commission-
ers under the Treaty of Ghent, gave to it the more poetic title,
Iris Island, but the earlier one was destined to prevail.

Judge Porter was one of the earliest settlers at the Falls,
having erected his first dwelling there in 1809–10.   He fore-
saw the unrivaled advantages of the position, and secured, at
an early day, the fee of a large tract of land in the vicinity.   In
addition to his dwelling, he erected mills on the site where
Lieutenant DePeyster built a saw-mill in 1767, and which
Stedman subsequently occupied for the same purpose.   He
also constructed a rope-walk for the manufacture of rigging,
for Porter, Barton & Co.,† who were then the principal carriers
over the portage, and owned or controlled nearly all the trad-
ing vessels on the two lakes and river.   All kinds of rigging,
and cables of the largest size required, were here manufactured.   Much of the hemp then used, was raised by the Wads-

---

* Those who visit Niagara in summer only, see but half its beauties.   In winter, the
spray, congealed by frost on every tree, bush and rock, glitters with diamond luster in the
sunlight; while, in the gulf below, cones, pyramids and towers, immense stalactites, and
frost-work in every variety of form, are produced by the falling waters.
† This well-known firm was composed of Augustus Porter, Peter B. Porter, Benjamin
Barton and Joseph Annin.

worths on the Genesee flats. Such was the scarcity of men in the then new country, that the Judge was indebted to Captain Armistead of Fort Niagara, for a company of one hundred men, to assist him in raising the heavy frame of his mill. It proved to be expensive aid, for the soldiers stripped his garden of all its fruit, then very fine and abundant. All his buildings, embracing dwelling, mills and rope-walk, shared in the general conflagration on the frontier, in 1813.

The village on the American side of the Falls, has been known as Grand Niagara and Manchester, and is now incorporated under the name of Niagara Falls.

Fort Schlosser was named after Captain Joseph Schlosser, a native of Germany, who served in the British army in the campaign against Fort Niagara in 1759.[*] Sir William Johnson found him at Schlosser in 1761. He must have remained until the autumn of 1763; for it is stated by Loskiel [†] and Heckewelder, that he arrived at Philadelphia in January, 1764, having just returned from Niagara with a detachment from General Gage's army. Heckewelder pays a high tribute to his humanity and manly qualities.[‡]

The earlier names of the post were, Fort du Portage, Little Fort and Little Niagara.[§] It was not built until 1750. In the summer of that year, the younger Chabert Joncaire, informed the Senecas that the French government intended to build a fort at the south end of the portage, above Niagara Falls. The project was carried into effect the same season, and we find that Joncaire Clauzonne, brother of Chabert, was appointed its commandant.[‖] In 1755, it was called Fisher's Battery.[‖‖] When Sir William Johnson invested Fort Niagara in 1759, Chabert Joncaire seems to have been in command at Fort Schlosser, his brother Clauzonne being then with him. On the

[*] N. Y. Colonial Documents, vol. x, p. 731, n. 5.
[†] Loskiel's Missions, p. 222.
[‡] Heckewelder's Narrative, p. 83.
[§] N. Y. Colonial Documents, vol. vii, p. 621.
[‖] Lewis Evans' map.
[‖‖] N. Y. Colonial Documents, vol. vi, p. 608, 706.

fall of the former fortress, Fort Schlosser was burnt, and its garrison was withdrawn to the Chippewa River, on the opposite side. It must have been speedily rebuilt by the British, for we find Captain Schlosser stationed there soon after in command of a garrison. The fort then consisted of an enclosure of upright palisades, protecting a few store-houses and barracks. Alexander Henry, who visited it in 1764, calls it a "stockaded post."* The plough has obliterated all traces of its existence, save some inequalities in the surface where it stood, plainly visible from the neighboring railroad. The tall, antique chimney which rises from the adjacent buildings, is not, as generally supposed, a relic of the fort, but of barracks, constructed by the French, and destroyed by Joncaire, on his retreat in 1759. The same chimney was subsequently used by the English when they re-established the post. The dwelling they erected was afterward occupied by Stedman, who was a contractor at the portage from 1760 until after the peace of 1783. He probably remained until after Fort Niagara was delivered to the United States by the British authorities in 1796, when he removed to the Canadian side. He left his "improvements" in charge of a man known as Jessè Ware. They are described by a visitor at that early day, as consisting of seventeen hundred acres, about one-tenth partially cleared, an indifferent dwelling, a fine barn, saw-mill, and a well fenced apple orchard containing twelve hundred trees.†

There appear to have been three brothers by the name of Stedman—John, Philip and William. The traveler Maude found John at Schlosser in 1800. While master of the portage, he accompanied the wagons and their escort, at the time of the massacre at the Devil's Hole in September, 1763, before alluded to. It was a return train, embracing about ninety persons, under the command of Lieutenant Don Campbell of the Royal American Regiment, which had been transporting

---

* Travels, p. 183.
† Voyage par Hector St. John, vol. ii., p. 153.

supplies from Fort Niagara for the use of the garrison at De-
troit. Only three persons escaped;—a drummer-boy, by the
name of Matthews,* who lodged in a tree as he fell over the
precipice; a wounded driver, who lay concealed in some ever-
greens near by; and Stedman himself, who, being well
mounted, forced his way through the Indians and fled amid
a shower of bullets, to Fort Schlosser. Two companies of
troops that were stationed at Lewiston, hearing the firing,
hastened to their relief. The wily Senecas, anticipating the
reinforcement, lay in ambush, and all but eight of the party
fell by the rifle or tomahawk. The entire garrison of Fort
Niagara were then dispatched to the scene, but arrived only to
find the ghastly and mangled remains of their slaughtered
comrades. The attack was made on the train while it was
crossing the small bridge over Bloody Run, so called after the
tragedy.

The Seneca Sachem, John Blacksmith, informed the writer
that the party which made the attack, were young warriors
from the Genesee, who, instigated by the French traders, se-
cretly organized the expedition under the leadership of Farmer's Brother, without the knowledge of their chiefs. Eighty
scalps, including those of six officers, were their bloody tro-
phies.

The Senecas, attributing the preservation of Stedman to
some miraculous interposition, and believing that he wore a
charmed life, conferred upon him the name of *Gä-nas-squáh*,
signifying *stone giant*. The story that they gave him all the
land lying between the river and the line of his flight, embracing about five thousand acres, is undoubtedly a fiction.
The pretended grant was the foundation of the "Stedman
claim," which was subsequently urged upon the State authorities with much pertinacity. If really made, it seems never to
have been ratified by the Senecas, for at a formal treaty made

---

* Matthews died in Canada, near Niagara, in 1821, aged 74.

with them by Sir William Johnson at Johnson Hall, in April of the following year, signed by Farmer's Brother and Old Smoke, it was not only not alluded to; but on the contrary, a strip of land four miles wide on the east side of the river, commencing at Lake Ontario and extending southerly to Gill Creek, embracing the entire Stedman claim, was ceded in perpetuity to his Britanic Majesty.* Stedman petitioned the Legislature in 1800, to confirm the pretended grant, but without success. He recites in his memorial, that he took possession of the premises in 1760, and soon after met with a great loss from the Indians; that as a compensation therefor, the chiefs gave him a deed of the tract containing 4,983 acres, which he had continued to improve for forty years; that the deed had perished with the papers of Sir William Johnson, which had been buried in an iron chest at Johnson Hall. A bill passed the Assembly, giving him the land he had actually improved, but it failed in the Senate. The buildings on the premises had suffered much from decay as early as 1800, and the adjacent fort was in ruins. The old orchard was still productive, the overplus yield bringing five hundred dollars in a single season; but the boys crossing from the Canada side, plundered most of the fruit.†

The Portage Road commenced at the Lewiston landing, and followed the river until it reached the small depression just north of the present suspension bridge. Diverging from this, it intersected the river above the Falls, a short distance east of the Stedman house, and followed its bank for about forty rods to the fort above. Midway between the house and fort, were a dock, a warehouse, and a group of square-timbered, whitewashed log-cabins, used by the teamsters, boatmen and engagees connected with the portage.‡

About half a mile below the Stedman house, near the head

* N. Y. Colonial Documents, vol. vii, p. 621.
† Maude's Niagara, p. 146.
‡ Manuscript letter of Hon. A. S. Porter.

of the present hydraulic canal, is the old French Landing, where goods were transhipped when only canoes were used, and where the portage road terminated before Fort Schlosser was built. Along the road, between the fort and Lewiston, block houses were erected about twelve hundred yards apart, to protect the teams from disasters such as had occurred at the Devil's Hole. The remains of some of these were quite recently in existence.

Judge Porter leased the Stedman farm from the State in 1805, the agent, Ware, being still in possession. He was ejected with some difficulty. Legal steps were taken, but owing to the unsettled state of the country and the difficulty of executing process in a region so remote from civilization, recourse was had to " Judge Lynch," before possession was finally obtained.* Judge Porter occupied the dwelling during the years 1806-7 and 8, when he removed to the Falls. He was succeeded by Enos Boughton, one of the first pioneers on the Holland Purchase, who opened a tavern for the accommodation of early visitors to the Falls, and travelers *en route* for the great West. It became the headquarters in all that region, for military musters, general trainings and Fourth of July celebrations. The buildings were destroyed by the British in December, 1813; but the old chimney was suffered to remain, conspicuous among the surrounding ruins, a weather beaten memorial of the ruthless desolation of war.

Gill Creek, so named from its diminutive size, and called also Cayuga Creek,† and Stedman's Creek, derives its only importance from being named as a boundary in some of the early Indian treaties.‡

Chippewa Creek, nearly opposite Fort Schlosser, is called by the Senecas, Jo'-no-dak, signifying *shallow water*; probably referring to an old fording-place at the mouth of the

---

* Manuscript letter of Hon. A. S. Porter.
† Savary s Journal, p. 360.
‡ Treaty at Canandaigua in 1794.

creek. Pouchot, in his narrative of the siege of Fort Niagara, calls it Chenondac, evidently the same name, and describes its banks as abounding in fine timber, suitable for ship-building.* It was named Chippewa, after the Ojibway—otherwise called Mississauga—Indians, who formerly lived on its banks. The Canadian Government by proclamation in 1792, gave it the name of Welland River, but it did not pass into general use. The earliest notice of the stream is found in the narrative of Father Hennepin, who, while seeking a site suitable for building the *Griffon*, encamped on its banks in the winter of 1678-9. He says, "it runs from the west, and empties into the Niagara within a league above the great fall." He found the snow a foot deep, and was obliged to remove it before building his camp-fire. The narrative incidentally mentions the abundance of deer and wild turkeys that were found in the vicinity.†

The Seneca name for Navy Island, Ga-*o'*-wa*h*-go-waa*h*, signifies *The big canoe island.* This is in allusion to the vessels built there by the French at an early day, for use on the lakes. Hence the French name, Isle-la-Marine, and the English name, Navy Island. It contains about three hundred acres. A tradition still exists among the Senecas that a brass cannon was mounted on one of the vessels.‡ It was there the French reinforcements arrived from Venango for the relief of Fort Niagara, during its siege by Sir William Johnson. The English built two vessels on the island, in 1764, one of which was accidentally burned there in 1767. The island has since become celebrated, as the rendezvous of the Patriot forces during the Canadian rebellion of 1838.

Grand Island is called by the Senecas, Ga-we'-not, signifying *The Great Island.* It is mentioned by Hennepin, under its

---

* Pouchot, vol. iii., p. 174.
† Hennepin, p. 75. Edition of 1693.
‡ A brass six-pounder was placed on one of the British vessels in 1764. Governor Simcoe's manuscript letter to Colonel England.

present name.* At its northern extremity, in a sheltered bay, the remains of two vessels may now be seen at low water, which, tradition says, belonged to the French, and were burnt at the time Fort Niagara capitulated, to prevent their falling into the hands of the English. This has given origin to the name, Burnt Ship Bay. I have been unable, however, to find any historical verification of this tradition. Sir William Johnson, while on his way west, in August, 1761, encamped for the night on the west side of this island, at the mouth of a creek now called Six Mile Creek, which he describes as a fine position, affording an eligible situation for a house, and a good harbor for boats. He called it Point Pleasant,—a name, the origin of which certainly entitles it to perpetuation. The Baronet makes special mention of the fine oaks with which the island abounded.†

Cayuga Creek was so named by the Senecas. In January, 1679, La Salle and his companions constructed a dock at its mouth, and laid the keel of the *Griffon*,—the first vessel built on our western waters. The site chosen was just above the creek, close to the river bank.‡

In commemoration of the enterprise, the name of "La Salle" has been conferred upon the small village and post-office at this locality. The same site was selected by the United States Government about the year 1804, for the construction of a small sloop of fifty tons burden, called the Niagara, which was used for conveying supplies to the western posts. The vessel was subsequently purchased by Porter, Barton & Co., re-built at Black Rock, and named the Nancy, after the wife of the late Benjamin Barton, one of the partners.§ While bearing the latter name she was commanded by Captain Richard O'Neil, and went out of commission just before the war of 1812.

---

* Hennepin, p. 49. Edition of 1696.
† Stone's Johnson, vol. ii., p. 45.
‡ A full account of the building of the *Griffon*, by the same author, identifying the site, will be found in volume i., page 253.—ED.
§ Mrs. Barton was usually called Nancy, but her baptismal name was Agnes.

Tonawanda Creek was so called by the Senecas, after the rapids at their village a few miles above its mouth, the name Ta-no'-wan-deh signifying literally, *a rough stream or current.* The French called it, " La rivière aux bois blanc," or "white wood river." On the early maps it is called Maskinongez, that being the Chippewa name for the muskelunge, a fish once abundant in the stream.

The Senecas have a different name for Tonawanda Island. They call it Ni-ga'-we-nah'-a-ah, signifying *The Small Island.* It contains less than one hundred acres. Its upper end having a fine elevation above the surface of the river, was an occasional camping ground of the Senecas, before their final settlement in this region. Philip Kenjockety (hereafter more particularly noticed), claims to have been born there, while his father's family, then residing on the Genesee, were on one of their annual hunting expeditions.

Two negro brothers lived at an early day, at the mouth of Cornelius Creek, just below Lower Black Rock. They were supposed to be runaway slaves. The elder was called by the Senecas, O-gah'-gwääh, signifying *Sun Fish,* on account of a red spot in one of his eyes, resembling that in the eye of the fish. Hence they called the creek, O-gah'-gwääh'-geh, *the residence of Sun Fish.* He was shrewd and intelligent; became a trader in cattle with parties in Canada and at Fort Niagara; chose a wife among the Seneca maidens, and acquired considerable property. The notorious Ebenezer Allen married one of his daughters, and added her to his extensive harem on the Genesee. The younger negro was called So-wak, or *Duck.* Both died more than half a century ago, leaving numerous descendants, some now living on the Tonawanda Reservation.[*]

Kenjockety Creek was not so named by the Senecas. They called it Ga-noh'-gwaht-geh, after a peculiar kind of wild grass,

---

[*] Life of Mary Jemison, pp. 124-129. Turner's Phelps & Gorham's Purchase, p. 406.

that grew near its borders. The name "Kenjockety," written in Seneca, Sgä-dyuh'-gwa-dih, was given by the whites, after an Indian family they found living on its banks. Its literal signification is *Beyond the multitude* John Kenjockety, the head of the family, was the son of a Kah-kwa, or Neutral Indian, whose father had been taken prisoner by the Senecas in the war which resulted in the extermination of his people. This occurred at the capture of one of the Kah-kwa villages, located on a branch of Eighteen Mile Creek, near White's Corners in this county. His family wigwams were on the north bank of Kenjockety Creek, a little east of the present Niagara Street. They obtained their water for domestic use from the river, then fordable at low water to Squaw Island. The creek still retains among the whites the name they first gave it—the Senecas adhering to the more ancient designation. The old chief must have been a man of more than ordinary consideration among his people. The Rev. Mr. Kirkland mentions him in the journal of his tour to Buffalo Creek in 1788. He writes his name "Skendyoughgwatti," and styles him "the second man of influence and character among the Senecas at the Buffaloe."[*] His name is appended to a letter addressed to Governor George Clinton in 1789, remonstrating against some unauthorized sales of Indian lands.[†] The Hon. Augustus Porter, who surveyed the boundary line of the "Gore," between the Seneca Reservation and Lake Erie, stated to the writer that he was accompanied during the survey "by an old Indian named Scaugh-juh-quatty," who had been appointed by the Senecas to act with Red Jacket for that purpose. They indicated the edge of the swamp as the line for Judge Porter to follow, by preceding him from tree to tree, thereby carefully excluding what is now called "the Tifft farm," and the remainder of the "Flats," as comparatively of no value. This will account for the zigzag course of the line in question.

---

[*] Kirkland's MS. Journal in N. Y. State Library.
[†] Hough's Indian Treaties, vol. ii., p. 331.

Kenjockety continued to reside on the creek, until about the commencement of the present century, cultivating his corn-field on Squaw Island, and drawing abundant subsistence for himself and family from the river and the forest. The survey of the "Mile-strip" by the State authorities, and the arrival of the pioneers of Buffalo, disturbed his tranquil home, and compelled him to remove to the Reservation, where he finally settled on the bank of Buffalo Creek, near the present iron bridge. Becoming dissipated in his old age, he perished miserably by the roadside, from the effects of intoxication, while on his way home from Buffalo in October, 1808.

Squaw Island was called by the Senecas De-dyo'-we-no'-guh-doh, signifying *a divided island,* referring to its division by the marshy creek known as "Smuggler's Run."* It was pre-sented by the Nation to Captain Parish, their favorite agent and interpreter, as an acknowledgment, says the record, of his many services in their behalf. The gift was ratified by the Legislature, in 1816, though the Captain was required to pay the State at the rate of two dollars per acre before he obtained his patent. He sold the island to Henry F. Penfield, Esq., in 1823. Captain Parish and his colleague, Captain Jones, had each previously obtained a donation of a mile square on the river, now known as the Jones and Parish Tracts, and lying within the present bounds of our city. The Legislature was induced to make this grant, by that touching and effective peti-tion dictated by Farmer's Brother, which has been so often cited as a specimen of Indian eloquence.†

Bird Island was originally several feet above the river level; rocky at its lower end, and partially covered with tall trees. Corn was cultivated on its upper end by Kenjockety's father. The island has entirely disappeared, the rock which composed it having been used in the construction of the Black Rock pier.

---

* Philip Kenjockety stated to the writer that he has often passed through this creek in his canoe, on his way to Canada.
† Copied in Turner's Holland Land Company Purchase, p. 291.

Its Seneca name, Dyos-dă-o-*doh*, signifies *Rocky Island.* It was called " Bird Island " by the whites, because of the multitude of gulls and other aquatic birds that frequented it at certain seasons.*

Black Rock being a convenient crossing place on the Niagara, became an important locality at an early day. Its history has been fully illustrated in an able and interesting paper entitled " The Old Ferry," read before this Society by Charles D. Norton, Esq.† Its Seneca name, Dyos-d.*iăh'*-ga-e*h*, signifying *rocky bank*, is a compound word, embracing also the idea of a place where the lake rests upon or against a rocky bank. Its English name comes from the dark corniferous limestone which outcrops at this locality, and, underlying the bed of the river, composes the dangerous reef at the head of the rapids.

Prior to the commencement of the present century, the usual route between Buffalo Creek and the Falls was on the Canada side, crossing at Black Rock. The Rev. Samuel Kirkland traveled it in 1788, and the Duke of Liancourt in 1795.

Fort Erie was originally built by Colonel Bradstreet, as a dépôt for provisions, while on his expedition against the Western Indians in the summer of 1764. It was located some distance below the modern fort. The part facing the river was built of stone, surmounted by squared pickets. The rest was stockaded. Bradstreet states in a letter to General Amherst, still unpublished,‡ that "when he arrived at the locality he found no harbor. That vessels were compelled to lie at anchor in the open lake, exposed to every storm, and liable to be lost. In addition to this, they were obliged to send more than twenty miles for their loading; that on examining the north shore, he found a suitable place to secure the vessels by the help of a wharf just above the rapids." "A Post," he adds, "is now building there, and all that can will be done toward finishing it this

---

* Campbell's Life of Clinton. p. 128.
† See vol. i., p. 91. En.
‡ Bradstreet's Manuscripts, N. Y. State Library.

season." He further says, that "to avoid giving offense to the
Seneca savages, to whom the land belongs, I have desired Sir
William Johnson to ask it of them, and they have granted it."
This letter is dated August 4, 1764. The treaty between Sir
William and the Senecas bears date two days after, at Fort
Niagara, and cedes to His Majesty all the land, four miles wide,
on each side of the river, between Fort Schlosser and the rapids
of Lake Erie. The islands in the river were excepted by the
Indians, and bestowed upon Sir William "as a proof," says the
record, "of their regard, and of their knowledge of the trouble
he has had with them from time to time." Sir William ac-
cepted the gift, but, like a good subject, humbly laid it as an
offering at the feet of his sovereign.[*]

The foundations of the present fort were laid in 1791.[†] It
must have been a rude fortification, as originally constructed,
for the Duke of Liancourt describes it in 1795, as a cluster of
buildings surrounded with rough, crazy palisades, destitute of
ramparts, covered ways, or earthworks. Outside of the fort
were a few log houses for the shelter of the officers, soldiers
and workmen. There was also a large government warehouse,
with an overhanging story pierced with loop-holes for the use
of musketry.[‡] The stone portion, the ruins of which still remain, was built in 1805, in the form of a quadrangle, and subsequently enlarged to more formidable dimensions. The Indian name of the locality, Gai-gwääh-gĕh, signifies *The place
of hats.* Seneca tradition relates, as its origin, that in olden
time, soon after the first visit of the white man, a battle occurred on the lake between a party of French in batteaux and
Indians in canoes. The latter were victorious, and the French
boats were sunk and the crews drowned. Their hats floated
ashore where the fort was subsequently built, and attracting
the attention of the Indians from their novelty, they called
the locality " The place of hats."

---

[*] N. Y. Colonial Documents, vol. vii., p. 647.
[†] Indian State Papers, vol i., p. 160.
[‡] Voyage par Liancourt, vol. ii., p. 4.

In the summer of 1687, the Baron La Hontan ascended, in his birchen canoe, the rapids of the Niagara into Lake Erie, on his way to the far West.* Appreciating with military eye this commanding locality, he recommended it to the French Government as suitable for a fort, and marked it " Fort Supposé " on the map which illustrates his journal. This is the earliest historical notice of the site of Buffalo. No attention appears to have been paid to the recommendation, and for more than a century it remained in undisturbed repose, its solitudes unbroken by the axe of the woodman, or the tread of advancing civilization. Voyageurs, traders and missionaries passed and re-passed on the river, but make no mention of even an Indian encampment. Nor does Sir William Johnson, who ascended the outlet into the lake on his way west in August, and returned in October, 1761.†

It has already been mentioned that the Senecas fled to Fort Niagara in 1779 before the invading forces of General Sullivan, and settled the following year on the banks of the Buffalo Creek. A single survivor of that fugitive band is now living on the Cattaraugus Reservation, in the person of the venerable Philip Kenjockety, a son of the John Kenjockety previously mentioned. When the writer saw him in June, 1864, he appeared strong and vigorous, being employed at the time in piling hemlock bark. His entire dress was a loose cotton shirt, and the customary Indian leggings. He presented a fine specimen of the native Indian of the old school, a class now almost extinct. He claimed to be one hundred years old, and a little examination into his personal history furnished proof of his correctness. It appeared that he was about fifteen at the time of Sullivan's expedition, and resided at Nunda, on the Genesee. He well remembered the flight of the Senecas on that occasion, when he drove a horse to Fort Niagara. The fugitives arrived there in the month of September, and remained

---

* La Hontan, English edition, vol. i., p. 82.
† Journal in Stone's Johnson, vol ii., pp. 451 and 470.

in its neighborhood and under its protection during the following winter. The season was the most inclement known for
many years; so much so that the river opposite the fort was
frozen from the seventh of January until the following March,*
and many of the Senécas perished from exposure and starva-
tion before the ensuing spring. Brant made strenuous efforts
during the winter to induce the Senecas to settle in Canada
under the protection of the British Government. The Mohawks, and a few from the other tribes, yielded to his solicita-
tions; but Kenjockety's father, who was intimately acquainted
with the superior advantages of Western New York, success-
fully opposed the Mohawk chieftain, and prevailed upon the
remainder to settle in the region watered by the Buffalo, Cattaraugus and Tonawanda creeks.

While listening to the eventful narrative of the aged Seneca,
the writer could scarcely realize that the man was still living,
who not only resided in this locality at the first advent of the
white man, but who came here, with the Senecas themselves,
to reap, by a permanent occupancy, the substantial fruits of
their ancient conquests.†

At the time of the arrival of the Senecas, the striking feature
of this locality was the predominance of the linden or basswood
over all the other trees of the forest. They fringed both borders of the creek, and spread their broad foliage over its fertile
bottoms. Seneca tradition tells us, that in the season when
the tree was in flower, the hunting parties from the Genesee
could hear, ere they reached the creek, the hum of the bee, as
it gathered, in countless swarms, its winter stores from the
abundant blossoms. Michaux, the French naturalist, who traveled through this region in 1807, states as a peculiarity of this
locality, in his great work on the forest trees of America, that
the basswood constituted two-thirds, and, in some localities,

---

* Merritt's MS.
† Kenjockety died April 1, 1866, aged over one hundred years.—ED.

the whole of the forest between Batavia and New Amsterdam.*
Early settlers say, that the peninsula bounded by Main Street,
Buffalo Creek and the canal, embracing what is now intersected
by Prime, Lloyd and Hanover streets, was almost exclusively
covered with this tree. It was occasionally found more than
eighty feet high and four feet in diameter. Its giant trunks
furnished, at that convenient locality, a light and soft wood
from which to fashion the Indian canoe, and a bark easily con-
verted into various utensils useful in savage life. This bark
formed the exclusive covering of the temporary huts, erected
for the shelter of the hunting and fishing parties that frequented
this region. The Senecas, in conformity with their well-known
custom, seized upon this marked peculiarity of the place, and
called it Do'-syo-wä, a name strikingly euphonious in their
tongue, meaning, *The place of basswoods.*

The origin of the name, Buffalo, has already been so thor-
oughly discussed in and out of this Society, that no attempt
will be made to throw additional light upon the subject. The
earliest occurrence of the name which I have been able to discover, is on a manuscript map in the British Museum, found
in a collection called King George's Maps, formerly in his
Majesty's library. It is dated in 1764, and embraces both
banks of the Niagara River from Lake Erie to Black Rock.
The American shore is represented as entirely unsettled, covered with forest and bordered with sand hills. Buffalo Creek
is laid down, bearing its present name. Its next occurrence is
in the narrative of the captivity and residence of the Gilbert
family among the Senecas in 1780-81, which was published in
1784. We next find it in the treaty of Fort Stanwix before
alluded to. The Rev. Mr. Kirkland, in his journal of a visit
to the Senecas in 1788,† speaks of their "village on the Buffaloe," and from that time the name appears to have passed into

* North American Sylva, vol. iii., p. 131.
† MS. journal in N. Y. State Library.

general use. The Holland Company endeavored to supplant it with the term "New Amsterdam," but our village fathers, with great good sense, rejected the substitute, together with the foreign names which the same Company had imposed upon our streets.

The Senecas, with a few kindred Onondagas and Cayugas, on their arrival here, in 1780, established themselves on the banks of the Buffalo Creek. The former chose the south side, and the level bottoms beyond the present iron bridge, east of what is now known as "Martin's Corners." The Onondagas went higher up, as far as the elevated table land, near where the southern Ebenezer Village was subsequently located. The Cayugas settled north of the Onondagas, along that branch of the creek which bears their name.

In these localities the tribes were found, when immigration reached them; and here they remained, dividing their time between hunting, fishing and the cultivation of the soil, until the encroachments of the white man diminished their game, and created a demand for their lands too eager and powerful to be resisted. We have seen, within a few years, the last of the Senecas abandon their ancient seats, on the confines of our city, some to locate on the adjacent Reservations, and others to seek "a wider hunting-ground" beyond the Mississippi.

They left the graves of their fathers in the possession of the white man, and how has he fulfilled the trust? A visit to their rude and neglected cemetery will furnish the answer. The grave in which Red Jacket was laid by his mourning people, is empty.* The headstone of the captive "White Woman," carried away by piecemeal, for relics, by the curious, no longer tells the simple story of her remarkable life. Pollard and Young King and White Seneca, and many others, whose names were once as household words among us, all rest in unmarked graves. They were the friends of the founders of our city,

* His remains were stolen by a Chippewa. They were recovered by his family and removed to the Cattaraugus Reservation.

when the Indians were strong and the white man weak. Those
conditions are now reversed. Having crowded the living from
their ancient seats and pleasant hunting-grounds, let us respect
the graves and protect the ashes of their fathers. One of their
eloquent chiefs, De-ji*h'*-non-da-weh-hoh, *The Pacificator,*
known to the whites as Dr. Peter Wilson,* has feelingly and re-
proachfully told us that "the bones of his people lie in exile in
their own country." Would it not be an appropriate work for
this Society, to initiate measures for the permanent preservation of their dead? The remains of such of their distinguished
chiefs as can now be identified, should be removed, with the
consent of their Nation, to our new cemetery. There, on the
quiet banks of the Ga-no*h'*-gwa*h*t-gĕh,† in the shadow of the
native forest, beneath the old oaks, where, within the memory
of the living, their council fires burned, and their war-whoop
rang,‡ under the same protection that guards the white man's
grave, they would rest in security, and the dust of our antag-
onistic races commingle undisturbed.

---

* He died in March, 1872.—ED.
† The Seneca name of Kenjockety Creek.
‡ Forest Lawn was owned, during the War of 1812, by Erastus Granger, then U. S. Indian Agent. His residence was north of the tall poplars, not far from the Main Street en-
trance to the cemetery. The oak grove near by, was used by the Senecas for their coun-
cils at that period. They were our faithful allies, and rendered us valuable assistance in
the contest with Great Britain.

APPENDIX TO THE FOREGOING ARTICLE.

The following list embraces many of the early names that have been applied to some of our great lakes and rivers, and to a few prominent localities along their borders. Several of inferior note, though of more local interest, are also given. The great diversity that has existed in the mode of spelling the geographical terms of the Iroquois, has given rise to much confusion and uncertainty. This has induced the writer to adopt, in reducing the Seneca names to English orthography, the admirable system invented by the Rev. Asher Wright, of the Cattaraugus Mission. That able missionary has published in the Seneca language, which he speaks and writes fluently, several works of much interest to the philologist, the fruit of his many years of successful labor among that people. The acknowledgments of the writer are justly due to him for his assistance in determining the orthography and signification of many of the names that occur in these pages; also, to Dr. Peter Wilson, Nathaniel T. Strong* and Nicholson H. Parker, all highly intelligent and cultivated members of the Iroquois family.

The following is substantially the key to Mr. Wright's system. If the sounds of the letters and accents are strictly observed, a close approximation to the correct pronunciation will be reached:

a sounded like a in fall.	o sounded like o in note.
ä sounded like a in hat.	u sounded like u in push.
e sounded like e in they.	ai sounded like i in pine.
ĕ sounded like e in bet.	iu sounded like u in pure.
i sounded like i in machine.	ch always soft as in chin.

Italic *h* sounded like the h in the interjection oh! when impatiently uttered; approaching the sound of k, though not quite reaching it.

When h comes after t or s it is separately sounded.

Italic *a* and *o* represent nasal sounds.

There are no silent letters.

A repeated vowel only lengthens the sound.

---

* N. T. Strong died January 4, 1872; Dr. Wilson, in March of the same year, and Mr Wright, April 13, 1875.—ED.

SENECA NAMES, WITH SIGNIFICATIONS.

Gah-dah'-gĕh. "*Fishing-place with a scoop-basket.*" Cayuga Creek, or north fork of Buffalo Creek.

Häh-do'-neh. "*The place of June berries.*" Seneca Creek, or south fork of Buffalo Creek.

Ga-e-na-dah'-daah. "*Slate rock bottom.*" Cazenovia Creek, or south fork of Buffalo Creek.

Tga-is'-da-ni-yont. "*The place of the suspended bell.*" The Seneca Mission House.

Tgah-sgoh'-sa-deh. "*The place of the falls.*" Falls above Jack Berrytown.

Jiihk'-do-waah'-gĕh. "*The place of the crab-apple.*" Cheektowaga.

De-as'-gwah-dä-ga'-neh. "*The place of lamper eel.*" Lancaster village, after a person of that name who resided there.

Ga-yah-gääwh'-deh. The Indian name of *Old Smoke*, who lived and died on the bank of Smoke's Creek. He led the Senecas at Wyoming. The name is now also applied to Smoke's Creek, and signifies "*The smoke has disappeared.*"

De dyo'-deh-neh'-sak-do. "*A gravel bend.*" Lake shore above Smoke's Creek.

Je-nya'-dih. "*The other side of the flats.*" Tifft's farm.

De-yeh'-ho-gä-da-ses. "*The oblique ford.*" The old ford at the present Iron Bridge.

De-yoh'-ho-gäh. "*The forks of the river.*" Junction of the Cayuga and Cazenovia Creeks.

Tga'-nou-da-ga'-yos-häh. "*The old village.*" The flats embracing Twitchell's farm. This is the site of the first village the Senecas built on Buffalo Creek.

Ni-dyio'-nyah-a'-ah. "*Narrow point.*" Farmer's Brother's Point.

Ga-noh'-hoh-gĕh. "*The place filled up.*" Long Point in Canada, and sometimes applied to Erie. In allusion to the Indian tradition, that The Great Beaver built a dam across Lake Erie, of which Presque Isle and Long Point are the remains.

Gah-gwah-ge'-gä-aah. "*The residence of the Kah-kwas.*" Eighteen Mile Creek. Sometimes called Gah-gwaä'-gĕh.

Yo-da'-nyuh-gwa*h'*. "*A fishing-place with hook-and-line.*" Sandytown, the old name for the beach above Black Rock.

Tga*h'*-si-yä-de*h*. "*Rope ferry.*" Old ferry over Buffalo Creek.

Tga-noh'-so-do*h*. "*The place of houses.*" Old village in the forks of Smoke's Creek.

Dyo-ge'-o*h*-ja-e*h*. "*Wet grass.*" Red Bridge.

Dyos'-ho*h*. "*The sulphur spring.*" Sulphur Springs.

De-dyo'-na-wa'-h. "*The ripple.*" Middle Ebenezer village.

Dyo-n*ah'*-da-ee*h*. "*Hemlock elevation.*" Upper Ebenezer village, formerly Jack Berrytown.

Tga-des'. "*Long prairie.*" Meadows above Upper Ebenezer.

Onon'-dah-ge'-gah-gëh. "*The place of the Onondagas.*" West end of Lower Ebenezer.

Sha-ga-n*ah'*-gah-gëh. "*The place of the Stockbridges.*" East end of Lower Ebenezer.

He-yont-gat-hwat'-ha*h*. "*The picturesque location.*" Cazenovia Bluff, east of Lower Ebenezer.

Dyo-e'-oh-gwes. "*Tall grass or flag island.*" Rattlesnake Island.

Dyu'-ne-ga-nooh'. "*Cold water.*" Cold Spring.

G*ä*hd*ä'*-ya-de*h*. "*A place of misery.*" Williamsville. In allusion to the open meadows at this place, which were very bleak in winter. *Blacksmith* says the name refers to the "open sky," where the path crossed the creek.

EARLY NAMES APPLIED TO THE GREAT LAKES AND RIVERS AND TO SOME OF THE PROMINENT LOCALITIES ON THEIR BORDERS.

LAKE ONTARIO.

Lac des Entouhonorons. Champlain, i. ed. 1632, p. 336. So called after a nation living south of the lake.

St. Louis. Champlain, ed. 1632. Rel., 1640–41, p. 49.

Lac Des Iroquois. Relation des Jesuites, 1635, p. 121.

La Mer Douce. "*The Fresh Sea.*" Relation, 1639-40, p. 130.

Ontario. "*Beautiful Lake.*" Hennepin, p. 31. Relation, 1640–41, p. 49.

Skanadario. "*Beautiful Lake.*" Hennepin, p. 42.

Cadarackui. Colden, xvi.

Frontenac. Hennepin, p. 40.

LAKE ERIE.

Erié. Relation; 1641, p. 71.
Lac Du Chat. " *Cat Lake.*" Sanson's Map of 1651.
Lac De Conty. Coronelli's Map of 1688.
Oswego. N. Y. Colonial Documents v., p. 694.

LAKE HURON.

La Mer Douce. " *The Fresh Sea.*" Champlain, appendix, p. 8.
Attigouantan. Champlain i., p. 324.
Karegnondi. Sanson's Map of 1657.
Lac Des Hurons. Relation, 1670–71, map.
Lac D'Orleans. Coronelli's Map of 1688.
Quatoghe. Colden, xvi.
Caniatare. Colden, xvi.

LAKE MICHIGAN.

Lac Des Puants. Champlain, 1632.
Lac Des Illinois. Relation, 1669–70. Marquette's Map, 1674.
St. Joseph. Father Allouez in 1675.
Dauphin. Coronelli's Map of 1688.
Michigonong. Hennepin, p. 53.

LAKE SUPERIOR.

Le Grand Lac. " *The Great Lake.*" Champlain, 1632.
Lac Superieur. "*Upper Lake.*" Relation, 1660, p. 9.
Lac De Tracy. Relation, 1667, p. 4.
Lac De Condé. Le Clercq, p. 137.

NIAGARA FALLS.

Saut d'eau. " *Waterfall.*" Champlain's Map, 1613.
Onguiaahra. Relation, 1640–41, p. 65. Applied to river only.
Ongiara. Sanson's Map of 1651. Ducreux, 1660.
Unghiara. Bancroft's U. S., vol. iii, p. 128.
Och-ni-a-gara: Evans' Map, 1755.
Iagara. Colden's Five Nations, appendix, p. 15.
O-ni-a-ga-rah. Colden's Five Nations, p. 79.
O-ny-a-kar-rah. Macauley's N. Y., vol. ii, p. 177.

www.ingramcontent.com/pod-product-compliance
Lightning Source LLC
Chambersburg PA
CBHW032142080426
42733CB00008B/1173